Outer Banks
impressions

photography and text by
Pat and Chuck Blackley

FARCOUNTRY PRESS

Front cover: With the ever-increasing tide of development overtaking the coastal areas of the East, the wild, rugged, and unspoiled beaches and dunes of Cape Hatteras National Seashore are appreciated and cherished now more than ever.

Back cover: Built in 1872, the Bodie Island Lighthouse is one of four historic lighthouses on the Outer Banks. Its restored Keeper's Quarters serve as a visitor center, run by the National Park Service.

Title page: Sunrise at Avalon Fishing Pier in Kill Devil Hills.

Right: In early morning, the placid waters of Silver Lake capture the reflections of Ocracoke's lighthouse and picturesque harbor.

Below: Up and down the Eastern seaboard, OBX decals can be spotted on everything from rusty old VWs to shiny, new BMWs, evidence of the Outer Banks' universal appeal.

ISBN 1-56037-352-0
Photography © 2005 Pat and Chuck Blackley
© 2005 Farcountry Press
Text by Pat and Chuck Blackley

For more information on our books write Farcountry Press, P.O. Box 5630, Helena, MT 59604; call (800) 821-3874; or visit www.farcountrypress.com.

Created, produced, and designed in the United States. Printed in China.
09 08 07 06 05 04   1 2 3 4 5

I must go down to the seas again, for the call of the running tide
Is a wild call and a clear call that may not be denied;
And all I ask is a windy day with the white clouds flying,
And the flung spray and the blown spume, and the sea-gulls crying.

— From "Sea-Fever" by John Masefield

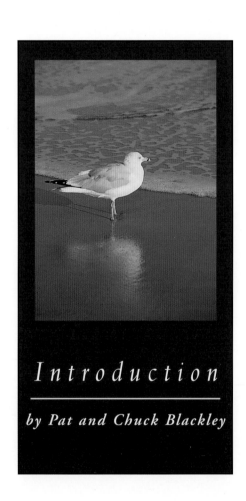

Introduction

by Pat and Chuck Blackley

For those who love the sea, Masefield's poem strikes a chord deep within their souls, evoking pleasant memories of quiet walks along wide sandy beaches, the smell of salt air and suntan oil, the sounds of children laughing and gulls crying, the sweet taste of ice cream cones and saltwater taffy, and visions of fiery-red sunrises and sunsets.

Nowhere are the sights, smells, tastes, and sounds of the seaside more intense than at the Outer Banks of North Carolina. No other place has such wide appeal or can arouse such passion and excitement. Just hearing the name can help soothe the stresses of modern life.

What is it about this place that makes it so loved by so many? What lures generations of devoted fans, with OBX decals proudly affixed to their vehicles, back to these shores year after year, ignoring those larger, glitzier beaches nearby? What gives the Outer Banks its distinctive allure and mystique?

Most believe the Outer Banks' mystique originates with its history. And what a history it is! English colonization in America began here, on Roanoke Island, when the first English colonists, sponsored by Sir Walter Raleigh, arrived in 1585. In August 1587, Virginia Dare became the first English child born in the New World. Unfortunately, this first attempt at colonization was not successful. By 1590, the entire colony of 116 men, women, and children had vanished without a trace, leaving a centuries-old mystery that may never be solved.

Adding an element of intrigue to the Outer Banks are accounts of the pirates who frequented the area during the early eighteenth century. They robbed ships, murdered their crews and passengers, and terrorized the island residents. The most notorious of the lot was one Edward Teach, better known as Blackbeard, whose reputation as a barbarian was widely known. But his reign of terror ended in November 1718 in the port of Ocracoke when the Royal Navy tracked him down, killed him, cut off his head, and hung it from the rigging of their ship.

Increasing the mystique are tales of shipwrecks along the windswept coast. More than 600 vessels met their demise here, earning the treacherous waters of the Outer Banks the moniker "Graveyard of the Atlantic." Among the ships in this watery grave is the ironclad USS *Monitor,* of Civil War fame, which sank in a storm off the coast of Cape Hatteras in 1862. Remnants of several wrecks are still visible around the islands.

Shaped like a long, bony finger protruding off of the coast of North Carolina, the inhabited islands that make up the Outer Banks (Roanoke, Colington, Bodie, Hatteras, and Ocracoke) stretch some 125 miles from the Virginia border to Ocracoke. They are separated from the mainland by wide, shallow bodies of brackish water called "sounds." This separation, and the fact that you must navigate a system of long bridges or take a ferry to get there, gives the Outer Banks a sense of remoteness, as if it truly is a world unto itself.

Bodie, Hatteras, and Ocracoke are fragile sand reefs known as barrier islands, and they act as a shield for the mainland, protecting it from the full force of Atlantic storms. Since they're made entirely of sand, the islands are continually on the move, shifting and relocating as the result of nature's barrage. Storms can create new inlets or close existing ones. Already narrow islands (less than half a mile at the narrowest point) may become narrower still. Thus, change is constant on the Outer Banks, and even for regular visitors, these changes may be evident from one visit to the next.

Incessant winds and dunes of soft sand are defining characteristics of the Outer Banks. These features brought the Wright Brothers here to test their flying machine, and, on December 17, 1903, they made Kill Devil Hill the site of the world's first controlled powered air flight. A memorial at this location now commemorates the historic event.

The adventurous are still drawn here today, with visions of harnessing those same winds. In Jockey's Ridge State Park, from atop the largest sand dune on the East Coast, people of all ages and abilities try their hand at hang gliding. Windsurfers and kiteboarders, including many of North America's top professionals in those sports, frequent the waters around the Outer Banks or even reside here.

But, without a doubt, the most popular sport here is fishing. Whether from the surf, a pier, or a boat, fishing rules on the Outer Banks. It's enjoyed nearly year round, although there are certain seasons when the big ones are running. And, while the sport is prevalent throughout the region, Hatteras tends to reign supreme for most anglers. Out past Cape Point, the warm waters of the Gulf of Mexico meet the cooler ones of the Arctic, creating a favorable environment for an incredible variety of fish species, and making this one of the world's premier fishing locations.

To many devotees, the heart and soul of the Outer Banks and the one feature, above all others, that makes it so special, is Cape Hatteras National Seashore, a unit of the National Park Service. Cape Hatteras, the nation's first national seashore, includes some 75 miles of unspoiled and undeveloped beaches, sand dunes, and marshes, plus three historic lighthouses. Within its boundaries, the Pea Island National Wildlife Refuge supports thousands of migratory birds and other wildlife. Cape Hatteras affords one of the last remaining opportunities to easily access and enjoy a wild and pristine seascape. This makes it a rare and unique treasure.

In truth, the Outer Banks doesn't have everything, but it comes awfully close. And, what it doesn't have, it probably doesn't need—for it possesses a balance of manmade and natural attractions that makes it ideal for just about everyone. Above all, it has a special feel. Even though it has developed over the years and has all the modern conveniences, it still feels like a small, kick-back-and-relax, Jimmy Buffet–kind of place. It's this feeling that remains with visitors long after they're back home and has them longing to return. And, they surely will return…time after time.

Right: At the Nature Conservancy's Nags Head Woods Preserve in Kill Devil Hills, five miles of trails wind through a diverse maritime forest ecosystem of ponds, swamps, wooded dunes, and deciduous hardwoods.

Far right: Built in the 1920s by wealthy industrialist Edward Knight and used as a hunt club, the Whalehead Club in Corolla is now the property of Currituck County. The mansion and its scenic grounds, located on Currituck Sound, are maintained as Currituck Heritage Park.

Left: Pea Island National Wildlife Refuge, on Hatteras Island, was established in 1937 to provide habitat for migratory birds and other wildlife. With a bird list that exceeds 365 species, the refuge is known as a "birder's paradise."

Below: After a long day of fishing, a lone seagull takes a break as the sun sets near Buxton.

Right: The Garden Clubs of North Carolina created the Elizabethan Gardens, on Roanoke Island, as a living memorial to the island's "lost colonists." The sixteenth-century pleasure garden is a showplace, with its flower-bordered walkways and antique statuary.

Below: Sorrel is prolific along the roadsides at Cape Hatteras National Seashore.

Descended from Spanish mustangs that were left behind by conquistadors more than 400 years ago, a small herd of wild horses still roams freely in the roadless region of northern Currituck County. This young colt is enjoying a snack of thistle down.

Canada geese find the grounds of Currituck Heritage Park a great place to raise their
families. These fuzzy little goslings seem to be enjoying the new spring clover.

Above: Sightings of whitetailed deer are common throughout the Outer Banks.

Left: At Fort Raleigh National Historic Site, this earthen fort is a reconstruction of the one built more than 400 years ago by the first English settlers in the new world. It was from this site that a "lost colony" of 116 men, women, and children disappeared without a trace.

Right: Currituck Heritage Park has 28.5 lovely acres on Currituck Sound for the public's enjoyment. Besides the Whalehead Club mansion, there are fishing docks, boathouse, footbridge, walking paths, picnic areas, and access to the Currituck Beach Lighthouse complex.

Below: From the top of Currituck Beach Lighthouse, you get a bird's-eye view of the restored keeper's house below, as well as the surrounding marshes, Currituck Sound, and the Atlantic. The awesome views make the climb up the 214 steps well worth the effort.

Left: Twilight casts a purple glow on the marina at Pirate's Cove, marking the end of another busy fishing day.

Below: A full moon slowly sets behind the Cape Hatteras Lighthouse.

Above: This curious turtle has come out for an evening stroll near Corolla.

Left: Because of its shallow shoals and fierce storms, more than 600 known shipwrecks rest off the coast or along the beaches of the Outer Banks, earning it the name "Graveyard of the Atlantic." Some of the wrecks are still visible, like the *Laura A. Barnes*, the ruins of which can be found on Coquina Beach at Cape Hatteras National Seashore.

Far left: The restored Chicamacomico Lifesaving Station in Rodanthe is now a museum; exhibits detail the heroic lifesaving efforts of brave men who battled the harsh forces of nature to rescue the crews of sinking ships from 1876 to 1954.

Above: Schools of dolphins, swimming just off shore, are spotted frequently by delighted beachgoers.

Right: Even man's best friend enjoys a morning romp with pals along the beach.

Above and left: Professional kiteboarder Dimitri Maramenides shows off his competition-winning moves at Kill Devil Hills.

Far left: A sunny afternoon at Kill Devil Hills finds hopeful fishermen at the Avalon Fishing Pier.

Left: While seabirds enjoy a late-day splash in a pond on Cape Point, the Cape Hatteras Lighthouse glows in the warm light of the setting sun.

Facing page: As dawn breaks over the village of Wanchese, fishing trawlers line the harbor, their rigging silhouetted against the painted sky.

Above: As dusk falls on Pea Island National Wildlife Refuge, the yellow petals of evening primrose begin to unfurl.

Left: In Corolla, the newly restored Whalehead Club mansion is a magnificent representation of Art Nouveau architecture.

Above: A lucky egret nabs breakfast.

Above: Inside Daniel's Crab House on the Nags Head–Manteo Causeway, crabs, hot from the steamer, cool as they are readied for patrons.

Right: Hidden away in a remote and roadless region of northern Currituck County, this lovely marsh is seen by few.

Far right: On an early morning ferry ride to Ocracoke Island, passengers leave their vehicles to watch as the ship slides out of the terminal at Hatteras.

At Cape Hatteras National Seashore, endless miles of unspoiled beaches are perfect for long walks or quiet introspection.

Left: Historic Corolla Village is the site of the original town center of Corolla. The village contains restored buildings from the 1800s, many of which now house quaint shops. The beautiful flowers and plantings in the Village Garden, located behind The Lighthouse Garden Shop, add to the charm of the village.

Facing page: Kids try their luck at crabbing at Currituck Heritage Park. Chicken necks tied to lengths of string make the perfect bait.

Right: The Hatteras Inlet Ferry transports visitors from Hatteras to Ocracoke. During the high season, the busy (and free) ferry runs from 5:00 AM until midnight.

Below: Near Duck, a windsurfer glides across Currituck Sound.

Facing page: Of the four famous Outer Banks lighthouses, the Ocracoke Lighthouse is the most southern, the oldest (1823), and the shortest (75 feet).

Right and below: At the North Carolina Aquarium on Roanoke Island, large viewing windows invite close-up examinations of myriad fish, mammals, and reptiles.

Right: The Outer Banks is known for its attractive beachfront vacation homes. PHOTO BY ROBB HELFRICK

Below: Hopefully these crab traps will soon be filled with those tasty crustaceans. PHOTO BY ROBB HELFRICK

Left: In the fishing village of Wanchese, a lifelong waterman prepares for his next excursion by mending his nets—a never-ending job.

Far left: Jockey's Ridge State Park, in Kill Devil Hills, contains the tallest natural living sand dune system on the East Coast. Hang-gliding is a popular sport here, and lessons are available for all levels of expertise.

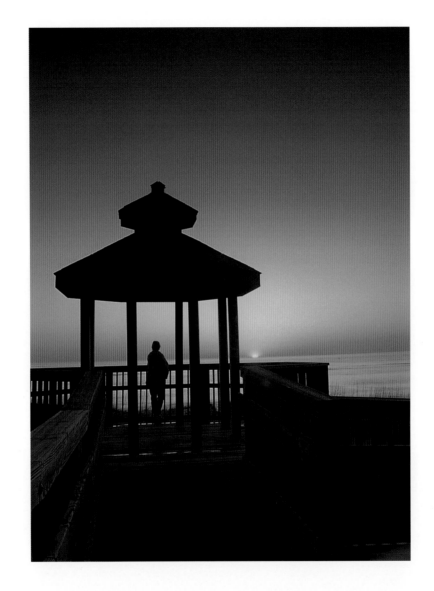

Right: A favorite entertainment at the Outer Banks is watching the sunrise, preferably with a hot cup of coffee in hand.

Far right: A fog-obscured sunrise at Kill Devil Hills.

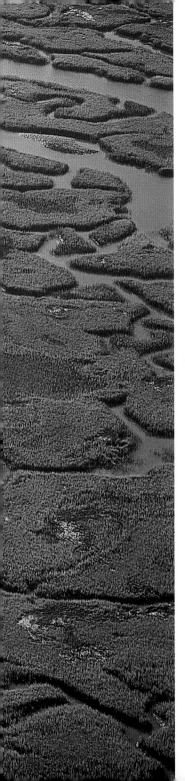

Left: From its favorite perch, a pelican watches the comings and goings in busy Ocracoke Harbor.

Far left: The artistic pattern of an Outer Banks marsh is unveiled by this aerial view.

PHOTO BY ROBB HELFRICK

As the last light of the day turns
the sky red, all is quiet at the
Bodie Island Lighthouse.

Right: At the Wright Brothers National Memorial, a 60-foot granite monument sits atop Kill Devil Hill, commemorating the brothers' first successful attempt at flight on December 17, 1903. Viewing it from an airplane seems only fitting!

Below: Blades of grass, whipped by the ever-constant and multi-directional winds, trace perfect circles in the sand.

Above: Always a part of the ocean scene, hungry seagulls circle the beach in their constant search for tidbits, either from the sea or from snack-toting beachgoers.

Left: The centerpiece of Roanoke Island Festival Park, the *Elizabeth II* is a representative sixteenth-century sailing vessel, similar to one that carried the first settlers to the New World. PHOTO BY ROBB HELFRICK

Right: A cluster of cattails makes a fine resting place for this little sparrow.

Far right: A boardwalk winds through the marsh toward the Currituck Sound. The Currituck Beach Lighthouse is in the background.

Below: You have to be observant to spot the wildlife in the Nature Conservancy's Nags Head Woods Preserve. This frog has positioned itself amid sticks and debris so that it's nearly invisible.

Surf fishing in front of a spectacular
Outer Banks sunrise. For dedicated
anglers, life just doesn't get any
better than this.

Right: A recent addition to Manteo's attractive downtown waterfront is this replica of the Roanoke Marshes Light, a screw-pile lighthouse that stood in the waters nearby from 1856 until 1955.

Below: Kids, water, and sand—all the ingredients needed for a fun day at the beach.

Above: Because of its favorable wind conditions, the Canadian Hole Day Use Area on Pamlico Sound in the Cape Hatteras National Seashore is a Mecca for windsurfers and kiteboarders. It was named in honor of the multitude of Canadians who frequent the spot.

Above: These soft-shelled crabs will soon bring smiles to some lucky diners' faces. PHOTO BY ROBB HELFRICK

Right: Great blue herons are regularly seen fishing along the shore at Oregon Inlet.

Left: Prominently displayed in the Visitor Center at the Wright Brothers National Memorial are full-scale reproductions of their 1902 "glider" and 1903 "powered flyer."

Above: Gaillardia pulchella, locally known as jo bells, are found in spring and summer along sandy roadsides.

Right: At the southern point of Roanoke Island, the tiny fishing village of Wanchese, with its boat-lined harbor, is one of the most picturesque locations in the Outer Banks.

Right, far right, and below: No matter what method you choose, riding the waves is a popular activity at Outer Banks beaches.

As morning breaks,
 the full moon sets
over Currituck Sound.

Left: The *Downeast Rover*, a 55-foot topsail schooner docked in Manteo, cruises at sunset in Roanoke Sound.

Far left: The North Carolina Department of Cultural Resources has proclaimed Corolla's wild horses to be "one of North Carolina's most significant historic and cultural resources of the coastal area." The Corolla Wild Horse Fund, a nonprofit group that works to protect and preserve this last known herd of Spanish mustangs, welcomes donations.

Right: At the Elizabethan Gardens on Roanoke Island, an azalea-lined walkway leads to a statue of Virginia Dare, the first English child born in the New World. Although she disappeared along with the rest of the "lost colony," the statue depicts her as a grown woman, based on local legends that suggest she survived and grew up among Native Americans.

Below: At the military Settlement Site at Roanoke Island Festival Park, costumed interpreters share what life must have been like for those first soldiers sent to the New World by Sir Walter Raleigh in 1585.

Left and below: Thousands of snow geese, as well as Canada geese, tundra swans, and twenty-five different duck species, spend winter at the Pea Island National Wildlife Refuge and the Bodie Island Marshes.

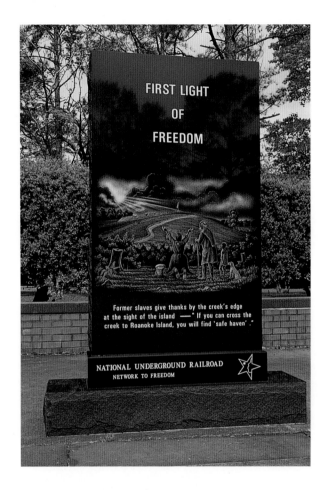

Facing page: At 208 feet in height, the Cape Hatteras Lighthouse is the tallest and, arguably, the most famous lighthouse in America. Threatened by tidal erosion that would have seen it toppling into the Atlantic, the revered beacon recently made history when it was moved some 2,900 feet to its new and much safer location.

Below: Someone was out for an early morning barefoot walk on the beach.

Above: Near the Visitor Center at the Fort Raleigh National Historic Site stands this memorial to the slaves who used the Underground Railroad to escape to freedom on Union-held Roanoke Island during the Civil War.

Left: The Oregon Inlet was opened during a hurricane in 1846 and was named after the first ship to pass through it, a vessel named *The Oregon.* Because of the shifting and migrating sands, constant dredging is required to keep it from closing.

Below: This busy trio is finding creative uses for sand at the Cape Hatteras National Seashore.

A vibrant sunset over Currituck Sound brings to a close another perfect day on the Outer Banks.

Pat and Chuck Blackley are a photographic and writing team from Virginia. Although they work throughout North America, their concentration is on the Eastern states. With a love of the outdoors, they find the mountains and coastal areas of the mid-Atlantic and Southern states to be favorite subjects. The Blackleys have enjoyed traveling to the Outer Banks for more than twenty years.

Their work appears in numerous magazines, including *Backpacker, Blue Ridge Country, Country, Endless Vacation, Family Fun, Frommer's Budget Travel, Outdoor Photographer,* and *Travel America,* and in books by Countryman Press, Farcountry Press, Frommer's, Insight Guides, National Geographic, Reader's Digest, and Ulysses Press. Additionally, their photographs appear regularly in calendars, commercial projects, and other publications by organizations such as Avalanche Press, Impact Photographics, KC Publications, National Park Service, Pace Communications, Sierra Club, Tide Mark Press, The Wilderness Society, and Willowcreek Press.

Their previous works for Farcountry Press include *Shenandoah National Park Impressions, Blue Ridge Parkway Impressions,* and *Shenandoah Valley Impressions.*